NAME YOUR EMOTIONS

SOMETIMES I FEEL HOPEFUL

by Jaclyn Jaycox

PEBBLE
a capstone imprint

Published by Pebble, an imprint of Capstone.
1710 Roe Crest Drive, North Mankato, Minnesota 56003
capstonepub.com

Library of Congress Cataloging-in-Publication Data
Names: Jaycox, Jaclyn, 1983- author.
Title: Sometimes I feel hopeful / Jaclyn Jaycox.
Description: North Mankato, Minnesota : Pebble, [2022] | Series: Name your emotions | Includes bibliographical references and index. | Audience: Ages 5-8 | Audience: Grades K-1 | Summary: "What does it mean to be hopeful? Feeling hopeful is an emotion everybody has! Children will learn how to identify when they are hopeful and ways to manage their feelings. Large, vivid photos help illustrate what hopefulness looks like. A mindfulness activity will give kids an opportunity to explore their feelings"— Provided by publisher.
Identifiers: LCCN 2021029771 (print) | LCCN 2021029772 (ebook) | ISBN 9781663972361 (hardcover) | ISBN 9781666325959 (paperback) | ISBN 9781666325966 (pdf) | ISBN 9781666325980 (kindle edition)
Subjects: LCSH: Hope—Juvenile literature. | Optimism—Juvenile literature.
Classification: LCC BD216 .J63 2022 (print) | LCC BD216 (ebook) | DDC 155.2/32—dc23
LC record available at https://lccn.loc.gov/2021029771
LC ebook record available at https://lccn.loc.gov/2021029772

Image Credits
Shutterstock: Africa Studio, 11, Andrea Slatter, 14, Brocreative, 19, Dean Drobot, 9, Decha Laoharuengrongkun, 15, Color Symphony, Design Element, fizkes, 12, GOLFX, Cover, photastic, 21(bottom), Rido, 7, Sellwell, 13, studiovin, 21 (top), Veja, 17, YAKOBCHUK VIACHESLAV, 5

Editorial Credits
Editor: Erika L. Shores; Designer: Dina Her; Media Researcher: Jo Miller; Production Specialist: Tori Abraham

Printed and bound in the USA. PO4608

TABLE OF CONTENTS

Words in **bold** are in the glossary.

WHAT IS HOPE?

Imagine you have a basketball game coming up. How do you feel? Do you really want to win? You are probably feeling hopeful!

Hope is an **emotion**, or feeling. People have lots of different feelings every day. Feeling hopeful makes you want to take action. You want what you're hoping for to happen.

WHAT DOES IT FEEL LIKE TO BE HOPEFUL?

Hope sometimes comes after a **negative** feeling. Maybe you are worried about a test at school. But you hope you will do well. Hope can help balance your emotions.

Hope can cheer you up. It's like a light at the end of a dark tunnel. If you are hopeful about your test, it can make you feel calm.

USING YOUR SENSES

Your **senses** help you to understand the world around you. Everyone has five senses. People can touch, taste, and smell things. They can hear and see too. Your senses send messages to your brain. That's where feelings start.

Imagine coming home after school. You see a present on the table. You probably feel hopeful that it's for you!

TALKING ABOUT YOUR FEELINGS

It's important to talk about your feelings. Sometimes a feeling is really strong. Maybe you have lots of different feelings. Talking can help you understand your emotions. Tell someone you care about how you are feeling. Explain why you feel that way. They can try to help you.

UNDERSTANDING HOPEFULNESS

When you are expecting good things to happen, you are hopeful. Hope is a **positive** emotion. It makes you feel good. You can be more creative when you are hopeful. You want things to change for the better.

If your grandma is sick, it can make
you sad. But you are hopeful she will
get better. Hope makes you feel better.

Hope can be a helpful emotion. It makes you a better problem-solver. It can also make you feel **brave**. When you are hopeful, you don't know what will happen. But you will find ways to get what you are hoping for.

Maybe your bicycle has training wheels. You feel hopeful that you'll learn to ride without them. This emotion pushes you to practice more. You feel brave enough to try riding without training wheels.

HANDLING YOUR FEELINGS

Some emotions can make you feel bad. Others can make you feel good. But it's OK to have different emotions. It's how you handle them that matters.

Feeling hope doesn't mean there will be a happy ending. Sometimes things don't turn out the way you want. That might be disappointing. But there are things you can do to feel better.

You can take a walk. Clear your mind.
Talk to a friend. You might feel disappointed.
But you can learn and grow from it.

You can help others to feel hopeful too.
If someone is feeling down, talk to them.
Be a good listener. Help them come up
with ideas to make things better.

MINDFULNESS ACTIVITY

Hope is a great emotion to share with others! This activity will help you spread your hopeful feelings.

1. Make a list of five people.

2. Write down kind wishes you'd like to send to each person.

3. Deliver the wishes. You can do this any way you'd like! You can have an adult help you mail or email them. You can drop them off. You can even call and read the wishes to the person.

GLOSSARY

brave (BRAYV)—showing courage and willingness to do difficult things

emotion (i-MOH-shuhn)—a strong feeling; people have and show emotions such as happiness, sadness, anger, and hopefulness

negative (NEG-uh-tiv)—harmful or bad

positive (POS-i-tiv)—helpful or upbeat

sense (SENSS)—a way of knowing about your surroundings; hearing, smelling, touching, tasting, and sight are the five senses

READ MORE

Jaycox, Jaclyn. *Sometimes I Feel Sad.*
North Mankato, MN: Capstone Press, 2020.

Nellist, Glenys. *Little Mole Finds Hope.*
Minneapolis: Beaming Books, 2020.

INTERNET SITES

KidsHealth: Relax and Unwind Center
kidshealth.org/en/kids/center/relax-center.
html?WT.ac=k-nav-relax-center

KidsHealth: Talking About Your Feelings
kidshealth.org/en/kids/talk-feelings.html?WT.
ac=ctg#catthought

INDEX

ABOUT THE AUTHOR

Jaclyn Jaycox is a children's book author and editor. When she's not writing, she loves reading and spending time with her family. She lives in southern Minnesota with her husband, two kids, and a spunky goldendoodle.